DRIFTING FOOTSTEPS

A Journey Through Love And Loss

CHARU GUPTA
AKSHI GUPTA

For the love that carries me through every chapter of life and stands beside me with unwavering faith, I dedicate this piece of my soul to you.

I LOVE YOU

Foreword

In a world teeming with countless stories, there is something profoundly universal about the journey of love and loss. It is an unspoken language, one that we all, at some point, understand. "Drifting Footsteps: A Journey Through Love and Loss" is not just a collection of poems but a mirror reflecting the most vulnerable corners of the human heart. These verses resonate with those who have loved deeply, hurt quietly, and sought meaning in the aftermath. This book is for anyone who has ever wondered if their emotions were too vast to contain—and discovered, through art, that they are not alone.

Each poem in this collection is a step along a path, a Drifting footprint that marks the passage of time, emotions, and memories. The words invite you to linger, to feel, and to remember. This book is a testament to the resilience of the human spirit and its capacity to love, even in the face of despair. It is my privilege to share this journey with you. Poetry, after all, speaks when words fail, and this collection seeks to amplify that silent voice within us all.

Preface

When I first began writing these poems, I did not set out to create a book. These pieces were born out of sleepless nights, quiet reflections, and moments when the weight of my emotions demanded release. They are fragments of my own experiences and, perhaps, echoes of yours. "Drifting Footsteps" came into being as I realized how interconnected we all are in our joys and sorrows, our questions, and our attempts to find answers.

This collection is divided not by chapters but by themes that flow into one another, much like life itself. From the purity of first love to the sting of broken bonds, from the chaos of overthinking to the quiet resolve of letting go, each poem is a snapshot of a particular moment or feeling. I remember one night, staring at a blank page when the thought struck me: "These words are not just mine. They belong to anyone who feels but cannot speak." That realization became the heartbeat of this book.

I hope that as you read, you will find pieces of yourself in these verses and that they will offer solace, understanding, or simply the comfort of knowing you are not alone.

Acknowledgment

No book is created in isolation, and this one is no exception. I am deeply grateful to the people who have walked alongside me, leaving their indelible footprints on my journey. To my family and friends who offered encouragement and support, thank you for believing in me when I doubted myself.

To the readers who will pick up this book, whether you stumbled upon it or sought it out, thank you for taking this journey with me. Your presence breathes life into these words. Finally, to the moments—both joyous and painful—that inspired these poems, I owe you gratitude. Without you, this book would not exist.

Prologue

The journey begins in silence. Before the first word is written or the first tear is shed, there is a quiet void where emotions swirl, nameless and formless. This book emerges from that void, a tapestry woven from threads of love, loss, longing, and resilience. Each poem is a footstep—sometimes confident, sometimes hesitant—on a path that winds through the landscapes of the heart.

"Drifting Footsteps" is not a story with a beginning, middle, and end. It is a collection of moments, each one capturing a flicker of emotion before it fades into memory. Love and loss are cyclical, much like the changing of seasons or the ebb and flow of tides. These poems reflect that rhythm, inviting you to embrace the continuity of emotions as they evolve and transform.

As you read, you may find yourself walking alongside the poet, retracing the steps of your own experiences, or perhaps forging new paths of understanding. Imagine each poem as a candle in the dark—its light may be fleeting, but it illuminates truths we often keep hidden. This is not a book that promises answers. Instead, it invites you to dwell in the questions, to feel deeply, and to embrace the beauty of the journey—even when it is fraught with heartache. Let us begin.

Content

1. Agape

2. Downpour

3. Echoes of First Love

4. A Love Too Vast

5. One Life: We Live We Die

6. A Love So Rare

7. The Beauty of Imagination

8. Cafuné: A Silent Promise

9. A Ride Through Time

10. Expectations

11. Is Life the Same for Everyone?

12. The Rise and Fall of Joy

13. Fractured Bonds

14. Fragments of Us

15. Sliding rope

16. Mind: The Enemy Within

17. Overthinking

18. The Silent Scream

19. Tears: A Flood of Emotions

20. Panic Attack

21. Life goes on?

22. Letting Go

23. Dead End

24. Story Of Silence

25. I Am Fine

26.   *Smile: Mask*

27.   *Life isn't the same anymore*

28.   *Echoes Of Emptiness*

29.   *The Play of Life*

30.   *The Scent of You: A Lingering Essence*

31.   *Lost in Her Fragrance*

32.   *A Dot: Afraid of Tide*

33.   *A Love That Came Too Late*

34.   *Tale of a Halted Love*

35.   *The Illusion of Healing*

36.   *Without you*

37.   *Isn't It Worst*

38.   *Strangers with memories*

39.   *Can We Fix Us?*

40.   *The Cycle of You: Drifting Still Forever*

41.   *The Battle of Love*

42.   *Stop, Before they fade*

43.   *What do I want?*

44.   *Writer*

45.   *Reader*

Agape

You're not bound to me—
You're a bird set free.
This isn't a trade; it's love's truth,
No chains, no debt, no need for proof.

All I want is to see you smile,
To watch you rise and conquer each mile.
You're above the world, radiant and free,
Chasing your dreams as they're meant to be.

From near or far, I'll always cheer.
Feel my voice, steady and clear.
Through life's storms, I'll calm your fears,
With love that grows through endless years.

Some may not understand this art,
How love can thrive with a giving heart.
But even in silence, it's loud and true,
It lives in the light I see in you.

They call it eros,
Where chaos becomes quiet devotion.
I gave myself to you,
Even as you kept me waiting.

I know this is more than just love—

It's a gift sent from above.

A selfless devotion, pure and true,

That seeks only happiness for you.

I love you, and always will.

No matter the distance, no matter the still.

Even if time should pull us apart,

You will always hold my heart.

Downpour

The clouds are coming down,
Becoming the mountain's crown.
Nature is a relief for the eye,
When it starts to cry.

Where the peacocks are dancing,
Children in the streets are playing,
Feeling reinvigorated,
Everyone's energy accelerated.

This isn't just a downpour,
But a rush of love to the core,
When everything starts to feel great,
With no room left for hate.

The rain whispers peace to the land,
Uniting hearts with a gentle hand.
Each droplet a blessing from above,
Filling the world with endless love.

The earth breathes deeply, renewed,
With every drop, it's like we're subdued.
A soft embrace, a fresh new start,
As the rain cleanses every heart.

Echoes Of First Love

You can never forget your first embrace,
A love that time cannot erase.
No matter where life's rivers flow,
A part of you still longs to know.

His face, a spark—a silent call,
A glance that makes the memories fall.
The laughter, tears, the dreams once made,
Like whispers that refuse to fade.

Though life has moved, the past remains,
A tender ache, a sweet refrain.
You're happy now, the path is new,
Yet something ties your soul in two.

First love may not end with bliss,
But leaves behind a gift like this—
A lesson carved in heart and mind,
A love once lost, yet undefined.

A Love Too Vast

When I hear your name, a smile appears,
Your presence stirs my heart with fears—
Not of loss, nor of despair,
But of love too vast to bear.

The blush on my cheeks is pure, so true,
Yet your smile, cruel in all it can do—
For with a glance, you make me weak,
A silent prayer my lips can't speak.

You are not just someone I admire,
You are the spark, the endless fire.
Not just a thought, but my only one,
The moonlit sky, my rising sun.

You are an essence of untold fiction,
A passion, an obsession, a sweet addiction.
The fragrance of love drifts through the air,
And in its whisper, I find you there.

This is not just a verse in rhyme,
It is devotion, beyond all time.
A letter to you, still unsent,
For you are the world I truly meant.

One Life: We Live We Die

One said,

"There are seven lives to claim."

The other spoke,

"Where multiverses flame."

Both declared,

"You can find them there,

But not in this life, Not anywhere near."

They painted worlds of endless light,

Of skies untouched by mortal flight.

But I know no realm beyond this breath,

No universe defies death.

Here, the air is sweet with rain,

A fleeting joy, a tender pain.

The sun ignites the trembling sea—

This fragile now belongs to me.

I won't let go of what I adore,

This life is mine; I need no more.

Someone said, "We live, we die,

No seven lives, no multiverse lie."

Why trade this love for shadows deep,
For dreams that may not cross my sleep?
This life is real; it burns so bright,
A fragile flame in an endless night.

If stars align in distant skies,
Or realms unfold when the body dies,
Let them wait—I will not depart.
This life is here; it owns my heart.

So think again before you stray,
Hold tight to what is yours today.
The stars can wait, the skies can shift—
This life alone is the greatest gift.

A Love So Rare

When tears of joy stream from his eyes,

A heart so grateful, reaching the skies.

He thanks the heavens for you, so near,

A love so pure, so crystal clear.

It fills your soul, yet stirs some fear,

To hold a love so rare, so dear.

A weight of care, a vow to keep,

To guard his heart, to never let him weep.

This is the love you've searched to find,

A bond is so true, so deeply aligned.

So cherish it now, let it brightly glow,

And never let this precious love go.

The Beauty of Imagination

That thought of you, a constant course,
A lifelong journey, love's true force.
The best part is imagining you—
Though far away, you feel so true.

Me and you, face to face,
Lost in your quiet, gentle grace.
Even in dreams, your glow shines bright,
Loving you feels just so right.

You're the love that lingers far,
A cherished ache, a chosen scar.
Amid the chaos, sharp and clear,
You are the voice I always hear.

Your laughter echoes in my mind,
A melody both sweet and kind.
Your touch—a whisper in the air,
A phantom warmth that lingers there.

The beauty of imagination stays,
A guiding light through life's maze.
I love you for all I am, all I lack—
The missing words my heart writes back.

No distance dims this love so true,

Even in thought, I am with you.

Cafuné: A Silent Promise

That small gesture, caught in mind,
A quiet wish you left behind—
A long glance, a silent plea,
The ache of love in reverie.

In the library, your heart sank low,
Love so near, yet left alone.
You watched them there—a gentle touch,
A fleeting moment that meant so much.

Yet in silence, you sat apart,
Hoping I will read your heart.
Wishing for my hands to soothe your hair,
Cursing fate for being unfair.

That unsaid need still lingers near,
A whispered echo, soft yet clear.
It stays with me, a fragile thread,
A silent promise, left unsaid.

And now, when fate lets us meet,
My fingers trace where longing speaks.
Through every strand, I mend with care,
Fulfilling what was left impaired.

A Ride Through Time

That friend I had from January to December,
The one in my dreams I still remember.
With a bike and all of my attention,
A bond so pure, beyond comprehension.

The friend who stood always by my side,
Always ready to give me a ride.
Yes, it was imaginary,
But we lived it like a story.

Now I can't see him; it feels like a dream,
Lost in the flow of life's rushing stream.
It's just that I've grown, left him behind,
But in my heart, he's still enshrined.

I wish I could be a child once more,
To hear his laughter, complaints, and lore.
Life was simple, brimming with creativity,
A world untouched by responsibility.

Back then, the days felt endless and bright,
Each sunset a promise, each star a delight.
No worries to burden, no weight to bear,
Just dreams in the wind and laughter in the air.

If only I could turn back time,

To days when joy wasn't a crime.

Now it's exhausting, being grown up,

Drinking from life's bitter cup.

Expectations

The word expectation,
Silently equivalent to disappointment,
Harms badly in a relationship,
That can't be healed even by ointment.

This is like a paper you crumpled,
Wanted only a person to unfold with love and care,
That unsaid thing you wished,
This is what expectation you're unaware.

When the paper was held by love,
Feel yourself in the sky and above,
When that paper wasn't even touched,
It hurt,
And if someone else notices the paper crumpled,
It becomes worst.

In the end,
When the paper becomes paper and is left for long,
You will feel so alone,
Those papers are still crumpled,
Makes you more hurt and dismantled.

And mark my words if someone said,

I don't expect anymore,

That means that when they did,

They hurt hell more,

Still what I did,

Expecting more and more ...

Is Life the Same for Everyone?

A crowd of many, yet you stand alone,
Some feel at home, while you still roam.
Laughter echoes, joy fills the air,
Yet deep inside, you're lost somewhere.

New friendships bloom, stories unfold,
Yet you hold on to memories old.
Some embrace the present with ease,
While you long for moments that bring you peace.

A warm meal for some, a struggle for others,
Some find comfort, while some seek covers.
Moving forward, chasing dreams,
Yet not all is as it seems.

Is life truly the same for all?
Some rise high, while others fall.
And those who feel this silent pain,
Know it's a battle, time and again.

The Rise and Fall of Joy

Happiness comes, so warm and bright,
Fills my heart with endless light.
But then a shadow starts to fall,
And joy is gone like it wasn't there at all.

I try to hold on, to keep it near,
But sadness whispers, loud and clear.
A thought appears, I don't know why,
And turns my laughter into a sigh.

I wish I could stop this sudden change,
But the harder I try, the more it feels strange.
Maybe the highs need the lows to stay,
Like night must come after the day.

Fractured Bonds

The mild airflow
Turned into a huge storm,
Took away the whole tree,
Leaving the stem and leaves free.

The leaves moved in their direction,
Seeking new affection.
The pain in the stem to let go wasn't easy,
Seeing the roots made it crazier.

For the roots were still there,
But the tree was nowhere to be seen, anywhere.
Symbolizing a broken friendship,
The whole tree once existed.

When two friends are apart,
One stood still while the other moved apart.
Though the roots still remained,
There was much fear, much pain.

But in the end, letting go is all that's left,
As life goes on, you must grow yourself.

Yaa...

We aren't friends anymore,

But the friendship remains pure,

And it's never truly gone.

Fragments Of Us

The glass falls,
Cracking all around,
Unites with a shattering sound.

When love and friendship break,
Thousands of cracks remain unseen,
A heart that screams, but nothing on the screen.

When there is love and friendship,
There is trust, there is communication,
But it unites with hardship,
Leaving behind a fractured foundation.

Some come into your life,
But not for your whole life.
It really hurts,
When you believe in a few,
And tell them to stick in life like glue.

Your faith is shattered,
For bonds once strong, now torn asunder.
Friendships, love—they change your perspective,
And leave you questioning what was truly effective.

The tears you hide behind a smile,
Pretending everything's fine for a while.
But the weight in your chest grows too strong,
And you wonder where it all went wrong.

The echoes of what was still linger,
A haunting reminder, pointing a finger.
You reach for something that's no longer there,
A bond that's broken, lost in the air.

Sliding Rope

Tears dropping,

My heart is paining,

Nothing feels good,

Unable to eat food,

Watching a sunrise,

Forgetting your real smile,

Pretending as much as possible,

Life being a hustle,

Want to lean on my lap,

You don't have one, feels like a slap,

Want to hold on,

Don't want to move on,

Wanna hold the sliding rope,

Want time to stop,

Nothing is the way you want,

It's only the pain you got,

It's hurting,

It's hurting,

But I have to live,

As promised to keep breathing,

Even though it's hurting...

Mind: The Enemy Within

I am a human who knows it all,
Yet when it hurts, I still recall.
The same thoughts return, piercing through,
Dragging me back to what I knew.

I know these thoughts will only sting,
But they circle back, like dirt they cling.
I hope to wake up and break this chain,
Yet my mind plays its game again.

Not the world—my mind's the foe,
First, it sings, its melodies flow,
Then it strikes, a slap in the crowd,
Where the shine in me hides behind a cloud.

It knows what's wrong, it knows what's right,
Yet it pulls me into another fight.
It always chooses the darker path,
And grins at me in its aftermath.

Yet in this war, a spark remains,
A voice that whispers through the chains.
"Rise above, don't let it win,
The fight begins from deep within."

I know it's not the world; it's me,

A curse etched deep in my destiny.

My mind toys with me endlessly—

It is my greatest enemy.

Overthinking

Dead memories become alive,

Creating the worst scenarios of life,

Making me dead a moment before,

And taking me back to life,

Riding this cycle always at late midnight.

Asking hundreds of questions,

Giving thousands of answers,

Even confused if it is reality or illusion,

And not having any conclusion,

Leading to anxiety and depression,

This is the worst situation,

Even with thousands of solutions,

You want an answer,

This is a disease even worse than cancer.

When someone left,

Telling yourself that I was not perfect,

After that, you make a distance,

Not to harm yourself,

But to protect others from this bad self,

And this is what the overthinking says,

You are a problem as only with you no one stays ..

The Silent Scream

The ones who scream, their voices high,
Soon I'll fall silent, too hurt to try.
When every word is cast aside,
They learn to smile, their pain to hide.

They beg, they plead, but all in vain,
Their cries dissolve like drops of rain.
The world ignores their quiet plea,
Their silence grows, a painful sea.

Inside, they long to break the chain,
To voice their hurt, to share their pain.
But silence wraps them like a cloak,
A shield against the words they choke.

Their screams are silent, yet so loud,
A storm concealed within a shroud.
It tears them up, it breaks their soul,
A battle fought they can't control.

The silence whispers, "Please take heed,"
But words won't grow where none will feed.
And so, they wait, in hope, in pain,
For someone kind to break the chain.

Tears: A Flood of Emotions

One with sorrow, the other with delight,
One in mourning, the other in respite.
One in struggle, the other in prayer,
One in anguish, the other in care.

One in panic, the other in peace,
One in turmoil, the other's release.
One in parting, the other in vows,
All drenched in feelings, each with its cause.

Not enough to overwhelm,
Not enough to douse the flame,
But a tide of reactions,
A thunderclap of the heart's own claims.

Tears are not a single drop—
They are millions of whispers,
Each holding a fragment of truth.

Panic Attack

Pain in my chest,
Hands that shiver,
An ocean of tears that won't rest,
Merging with sweat that quivers.

The coordination of my body breaks,
It feels like the end,
Then suddenly, I wake—
From the nightmare, I can't pretend.

I realize it was just another failure,
A death stare, silent and cold,
Where pain, tears, and sweat unfold,
But the panic... still takes its toll.

The silence screams louder than before,
Each breath a battle I can't ignore.
The storm inside, it doesn't cease,
Longing for a moment of peace.

Life Goes On?

Life Goes On

The river flowed endlessly, free,

Like a wanderer in joyful spree.

But one day, midway along,

A dam appeared, and joy felt wrong.

Happiness now seemed a fleeting scam,

Water held still by the cold, hard dam.

Emotions muted, no forced display,

The river mourned its blissful way.

It longed for magic, for the elf,

To help reclaim its joyful self.

Pressure built in silent streams,

Until one day, it burst through dreams.

The river surged, a fearless cry,

Yet something lingered—an inward sigh.

Back in motion, it carried on,

But something precious now seemed gone.

Gleeful moments, left behind,

A shadow of fear etched in its mind.

Flowing forward, forced to strong,

Because, as they say, "Life goes on."...

Letting Go

A silent voice or a shouting heart,
Smiles on lips while the tears quietly start.
The world moves on, yet my soul stays still,
Chained to the memories against my will.

A bright moon shines behind a cloudy veil,
Like hope trying to bloom in a stormy gale.
Every step forward feels like a retreat,
For the echoes of us are impossible to beat.

I long to hold on, just a little more,
But life whispers, "Let go, there's more in store."
Yet how do I leave when my heart remains,
Tied to a love that still courses through my veins?

Sleepless nights stretch endlessly wide,
Haunted by dreams where we stand side by side.
I see us smiling, lost in our fights,
A bittersweet dance under fractured lights.

They say dying is the hardest part,
But they've never known the ache of a breaking heart.
To let go of someone you called your own,
Is to wander the world forever alone.

Tell me, how do I mend what's been torn apart,

When the world says "move on," but I left my heart?

64

Dead End

Forever came to an end,

Hoping for time to expand.

Promises left undone,

Memories that can't be forgotten,

All tangled into a web of thoughts,

That we are no longer friends anymore.

The only question remains:

How many lessons still await in addition?

Turning my favourites into lessons,

Or am I just so bad that I can't hold friends?

But I can't hold anything,

Because the bond has dissolved, left like nothing.

And finally,

Forever came to an end,

Leaving me at a dead end.

Story Of Silence

It's hard to breathe,
It's hard to scream.
When the heartbeat quickens,
The tears freeze.

The lips hold a smile,
While inside, you're about to die.
Still, when someone asks,
You say, "I am fine,"
With a strong smile, like aged wine.

Where the heart screams, "No,"
But the brain says, "Let go."
As you've learned, it's better to let go,
Because no one is there when you need them most.

Behind the smile, there's a void,
A silence that can't be destroyed.
You've mastered the art of pretending,
But deep inside, you're never mending.

You carry the weight, you bear the pain,
Hoping one day, you'll be free again.

And so you walk this endless road,

Heavy with the burden you've been told,

To carry alone, with no reprieve,

While everyone around you seems to leave.

Yet still, you wear your mask so bright,

Hiding the storm, hiding the fight.

I Am Fine

Listening to the whole world,

Without uttering a word,

Filled with a lot,

Yet hiding your inner thought.

Leading to concealment,

An emotional detachment,

It's a horde,

But still, it feels alone.

Surrounded by the crowd,

Yet silence wraps you like a shroud.

It becomes your enemy,

Overthinking like a praying deity.

Yeah...

A lot is going on inside,

Yeah...

A lot is going on inside.

But whenever someone asks...

I smile,

Every time, I reply the same,

"Yeah... I am fine."

I am fine...

Smile: Mask

When I start living life,

I no longer feel alive.

With forever suffering,

They say, "Keep smiling."

Then,

A smile on my face,

Tears in my eyes,

Searching for a small space,

To shout and cry.

Everyone says...

One day, it will heal,

Unaware of how it feels,

Unseen is my scream,

Where death feels better than this awful dream.

One thing I want to ask,

Why do I have to wear this mask...

Why?

Why?

Why?

Behind the mask, I'm trapped inside,

Fighting battles I cannot hide.

The world sees only what I show,

But they don't know the pain below.

Life Isn't the Same Anymore

Life isn't the same anymore,
Becoming dull, more and more.
No special breakfast on a Sunday,
Making it no longer a special day.

No more casual chats with my parents,
As we're too busy with life's errands.
Even talking to my siblings feels like a chore,
Changing life's rhythm, from what it was before.

From daily fight's to barely a word,
Not even a glance, though we're all in the same world.
I wait for a long weekend to come,
Or the end of the month to finally be done.

Their happiness is my guiding light,
But I wonder where my joy took flight.
Who says adulthood is so grand?
I long for the childhood I once had.

Life isn't the same anymore,
Becoming dull, more and more.

Echoes Of Emptiness

What to do with the constellation
When all I long for is an ocean?
Hope you're happy, far from me,
While I've lost my happiness's key.

The moon follows me on its trail,
Yet darkness looms where stars grow pale.
A rainbow shines, but the sea is gone—
What's light worth if its warmth is withdrawn?

Yes, I survive without your touch,
If breathing is "living," though it's not much.
Dreams now drift like ships untethered,
Lost in storms that can't be weathered.

The Play Of Life

Everything will be okay,
But life feels like a play.
Where everyone says, "Be strong,"
"There's nothing wrong."

But deep down, you want to be happy,
Not just hearty.
You want to talk, you want to smile,
But pretending becomes your life.

You know you can't do anything,
But your heart wants to do everything.
You're holding your emotions tight,
Leading yourself into your own fight.

As now, you don't feel yourself,
That pain inside becomes the "new self."
Everything will be okay,
But life feels like a play.

The Scent of You:
A Lingering Essence

The fragrance of you is beyond compare,
More soothing than blossoms perfuming the air.
You don't know your worth, how rare you are,
Outshining the glow of a billion stars.

I hug you to hold your scent so near,
It lingers on me, soft and clear.
My clothes now carry your sweet perfume,
A trace of you in every room.

The hoodie I wore when we last embraced,
I've kept it untouched, perfectly placed.
Its threads still hold your tender smell,
Reviving memories I know too well.

Your scent's a map, a trail to you,
A guide through days when skies aren't blue.
It whispers of moments, both fleeting and true,
A melody played by the essence of you.

Each breath I take feels bittersweet,
A memory clings, but we're incomplete.

Your absence echoes, yet you're so near,
Through the scent you left, I hold you here.

If only the wind could carry my plea,
And bring back your warmth, your touch to me.
For now, I'll wear this hoodie tight,
To dream of you in the quiet night.

Your gaze, your essence, your warm embrace,
Nothing on earth could ever be replaced.
When I miss you, I breathe you in deep,
Your scent, is a comfort that helps me keep.

I wear the hoodie to feel you again,
But it also reminds me of bittersweet pain.
For though your fragrance fills my space,
It can't replace your missing face.

I miss you still, more than I can say,
Your scent is here, but you're far away.

Lost In Her Fragrance

A man, entranced by her fragrant air,
A spell so sweet, beyond compare.
He breathes her in, and time stands still,
A captive to her tender will.

Her essence lingers, soft and pure,
A memory he longs to endure.
In her embrace, he forgets the place,
Lost in the scent, her unseen trace.

When she wears his clothes, they hold her hue,
A perfume that feels both old and new.
He keeps them close, won't let them fade,
A treasure in her scent, lovingly made.

Oh, how he yearns to be surrounded,
By that fragrance where his love is grounded.
Forever lost, yet always found,
In her essence, where his heart is bound.

A Dot: Afraid Of Tide

A million thoughts, a single dot,

One day, how everything just stopped.

Emotions once shared now feel like a weight,

A burden too heavy, yet sealed by fate.

We once shared these dots, a silent link,

Instantly knowing what the other might think.

But now, the silence grows and binds,

A deepening crack between our minds.

These aren't just dots; they're little boats,

Sailing oceans with trembling hope.

They have a destination but fear the waves,

Afraid to love, afraid to be brave.

Waves of longing, waves of doubt,

Waves that scream, "Don't let it out."

Waves of pretending, "I'm just fine,"

Waves of masking behind a smile's line.

I still see your dot, its meaning clear—

It whispers the words I long to hear:

"I miss you. I want you. I need you.

Stay by my side, I love you."

But all you say is the silent dot,

And knowing the truth, I still ask, "What?"

I hope someday this quiet will break,

Your emotions, not just dots, will finally awake.

One day, when the moon will call,

A tide in you will rise and enthrall.

The waves will calm, the boats will land,

And love will bloom on the golden strand.

No more dots, just emotions that flow—

Not tears of sorrow, but a joy to show.

I'll wait for you to become my moon,

Until our dots fade, and hearts attune.

A Love That Came Too Late

I'll never forget the white hoodie he wore,

The first time I saw him, I couldn't ignore.

Mature and calm, he caught my eye,

And from that moment, my heart learned to fly.

Months of talking, now face-to-face,

I saw his love, though hidden in grace.

He cared for me but struggled to show,

While I gave my all, hoping he'd grow.

Three years passed, the same old refrain,

I longed for his love but waited in vain.

It wasn't hate, just a Drifting light,

Yearning for warmth in the cold of night.

When I was ready to let it all go,

He started to change, his feelings to show.

But by then, my world had begun to shift,

And the love we had was adrift.

To save us both from further pain,

I chose to walk away, though it felt insane.

Four years of love, now left behind,

A bittersweet memory etched in my mind.

I miss him still, but strength must stay,

For moving on is the only way.

Some love lingers, though lives move apart,

Forever a piece of him stays in my heart.

Tale of a Halted Love

Never thought I could love like that,

Don't know how I stuck like that,

Somehow attached all my strings,

Now detaching it hurts like pins.

We won't be together next to each,

Yet the feelings will stand stitched,

The safest and special place you hold,

Both in my heart and my soul.

Let me express one more time, so,

Come to me when you find no one.

Come to me when you need someone.

Come and give your deepest adversity.

Come and take happiness in exchange.

That's the trade I would love to do.

That's the path I would choose to go.

The Illusion of Healing

Healing feels like clever lies,
A mask I wear with hollow eyes.
I hide the tears, suppress the pain,
Yet echoes call me once again.

They say that time will mend the ache,
Yet some wounds never seem to break.
The scars remain, the past still calls,
A whisper trapped within these walls.

I fake a smile, I move ahead,
Yet something's missing, left unsaid.
The days feel light, the nights too long,
Like lyrics lost inside a song.

I tell myself the pain is gone,
Yet shadows haunt me all night long.
I push, I run, I try to mend,
But wounds don't heal—they just pretend.

You numb the hurt, ignore the sting,
Hoping it won't change a thing.
You call it healing, yet inside,
You're just a ghost you try to hide.

Without You

Spending the day is easy,

But the nights are crazy.

When the heart starts ruling the brain,

All your memories and voice swirl in vain.

It's hard to think,

When every emotion begins to sink.

All understanding fades away,

As I let out the pain I can't convey.

Please, tell me how to spend the nights,

When it feels like I'm spending my whole life,

Without you...

The darkness whispers your name,

And nothing feels the same.

Each moment is a reminder, a cruel replay,

Of the love that's now far away.

I search for you in every dream,

But the silence only makes me scream.

The nights stretch long, like endless roads,

While my heart carries all these heavy loads.

Isn't It Worst

A smiling face, tears in the eyes,

Even after holding back when you cry.

Isn't it the worst,

When you're filled with emotions, yet can't say a word?

When you understand everyone,

But for you, there's no one.

Isn't it the worst,

When in the end, you feel like you're worth zero?

Holding your emotions tight,

And suffocating, it leads to destruction's bite.

Isn't it the worst,

When everything feels like a curse?

There's a storm inside,

But no words to confide.

Isn't it the worst,

When the poet is left with zero words?

Strangers With Memories...

We were always there to listen,

Together we had so much fun.

We were friends,

Promised that it would never end.

All those moments are now stories,

Now, we are strangers with memories.

When I see two friends standing close,

It genuinely hurts,

Getting a déjà vu,

And remembering how everything got screwed.

Realizing the forever friendship had ended,

Forgotten like it never existed.

In the end, I realize,

I, being a diamond, was treated like coal in a mine.

The laughter we shared, now gone,

The bond we built, is now undone.

And though I try to move on,

The echo of our love and friendship lingers on.

I search for closure in space,

Trying to forget your familiar face.

But every corner still holds a trace,

Of the love I can't replace.

Can We Fix Us?

You said it would last forever,
That nothing could part us, ever.
I want this to be hand in hand,
Not just a dream in some distant land.

I want a life full of new memories,
Not one spent living with old reveries.
It's not about moments between a few—
All I want, all I need, is you.

I know time has the power to change,
But we aren't something to rearrange.
You live in every breath I take,
You taught me life's depth, for my sake.

I know we've stumbled, faced the fall,
But love can rise above it all.
Through cracks, the strongest bonds are made,
In every shadow, light invades.

Yes, I'll do whatever you ask,
Even if it's the hardest task.
But I want us together, strong,
Not broken, not where hearts don't belong.

I'm letting you go because you wish,
But deep inside, it feels amiss.
One question lingers, steady and clear:
Can we please fix what brought us here?

Remember we promised, didn't we say,
We'd walk together, come what may?
Everything can heal, can be made right—
If only we choose to hold on tight.

The Cycle of You: Drifting Still Forever

Filled with hope, I think I'll move on,
Survive the day, though you're still gone.
But the first thought that comes to mind,
Is you—so hard to leave behind.

I smile throughout the day, a mask I wear,
To hide the pain, the quiet despair.
I pray for strength, I tell myself,
"I'm stronger than this, I'll find myself."

Then someone asks, "Are you okay?"
And keeping that smile feels far away.
With a soft reply, "Yes, I'm alright,"
But deep inside, I'm lost in the night.

Then comes the time when I let it go,
Surrender my heart, let the tears flow.
The pillow wipes away my pain,
The bedsheet wraps me once again.

With a smile, I drift into the past,

Lost in memories that never last.

I dream of you, though you're not near,

And the cycle repeats, year after year.

But with each new dawn, I fight the same fight,

Chasing the day, avoiding the night.

Yet in every shadow, I still see your face,

A silent reminder, a soft embrace.

The Battle of Love

The sun ascends, painting the skies with gold,

Yet mornings now feel distant, cold.

I reach for my phone, a habit ingrained,

But your message is gone, only silence remains.

Your voice once greeted me every dawn,

Now I rise to emptiness, feeling withdrawn.

I replay your words, your laughter, your tone,

Yet each passing day leaves me more alone.

Through the hours, I long for your face,

A love so deep, no one could replace.

I imagine your touch, your hand in mine,

But reality strikes—I'm far from fine.

In dreams, we wonder where time doesn't end,

Two hearts as one, no need to pretend.

But waking cuts deeper, the ache feels new,

For mornings arrive, and I'm without you.

Your name lingers in every thought I find,

A melody playing on a loop in my mind.

I hope you'll see, when the battles are done,

That losing me means losing the one.

I wish you'd feel my love through the pain,

Through sleepless nights and the falling rain.

No words can explain this void you've left,

A heart once whole now feels bereft.

One day, I pray, the truth will shine,

You'll realize my love was always divine.

And in that moment, under the sun,

You'll call for me and say my love your love won.

Stop, Before They Fade

The ocean sighed, its voice so deep,

"Why do I give, yet none shall keep?"

"I offer waves, embrace the shore,

Yet they take and still want more."

The tree stood tall and softly swayed,

"I know your pain," it gently said.

"I give them shade, a place to rest,

Yet they forget though I give my best."

"I lift the air so they can breathe,

I stand through storms, yet they still leave."

"Why does love that's freely shown

Feel unseen, left all alone?"

The ocean wept, the tree stood still,

Yet both kept giving, against their will.

Not for return, nor acclaim,

But because they loved, despite the pain.

Then the human paused and saw anew,

The love is so constant, deep, and true.

"The fault is mine," they whispered low,

"I failed to cherish what won't let go."

"For love like this is rare to find,
A heart that gives, yet stays behind."
"Before regret becomes my chain,
I'll hold them close, I won't refrain."

So, love the ones who give their all,
Before they fade, before they fall.
For oceans to recede and trees will bend,
And even the strongest hearts can end.

Cherish the love that does not stray,
For once it's gone, it won't remain.

What Do I Want?

The morning message with a heart,
Your smile, a masterpiece of art.
The unasked updates, soft and true,
A quiet reminder—someone cares for you.

That call, effortless and free,
Where life felt light, like waves at sea.
The smiling us, side by side,
Where life was kind, no need to hide.

The simple Have you eaten yet?
A love so constant, without regret.
The little gestures, pure and bright,
Where life felt warm, where all was right.

The days I felt at home,
The nights I was never alone.
Every message, every call,
Made the world fade—I had it whole.

A life wrapped in you,
A day soaked in your essence too.
Not just in thoughts,
But in the presence of you.

"What do you want?"—you ask me so.

But the answer, love, you already know.

All I seek, all I know—

It's just you.

Writer

The writer ..

The word lover ...

Now I'm afraid of words ..

Emotions feel like a curse ...

Pain drifts with each word ..

Distancing from the world ...

Fighting a battle to write ..

Aware of tears dripping after the fight ...

Afraid of what you love ..

Afraid of what you are ...

Hating yourself is what you got ..

Hold every word with dots ...

Dot of unsaid words ..

The unfought wars ...

The writer is no longer a writer ..

It's just an ordinary person who is a failed lover ...

Reader

Your story matters too.

*Now it's your turn to speak out and tag me at **@writer_insan**.*

Afterword: A Reflection on The Journey

As I sit back and reflect on the journey that has unfolded through these poems, I find myself caught between moments of clarity and chaos. Each word, each verse, feels like a stepping stone—a part of a larger path that spirals through love, loss, pain, and healing. "Drifting Footsteps: A Journey Through Love and Loss" is not just a collection of poems; it is a map of the emotional landscape I've traversed and shared with you, the reader.

This journey has not been linear. It has been messy, raw, and sometimes dark, but it has also been filled with fleeting moments of light. From the passionate love explored in "Agape" and "A Love So Rare" to the heart-wrenching pain found in "Tears: A Flood of Emotions" and "The Silent Scream," I have bared pieces of myself within each line. These poems have been both a form of catharsis and a way to connect with you, the reader, on a deeply human level.

Some of these poems were written in the quiet of despair, others in the frenzy of overthinking and longing. But in each one, I found the courage to speak truths—about love, loss, self-doubt, and healing. There were times when the words felt impossible to capture, and yet, through persistence, they emerged in ways that surprised me.

In "The Play of Life," I examined the constant dance between joy and sorrow, and in "Fractured Bonds," I confronted the breaking of connections that seemed unshakable. In "Life Isn't the Same

Anymore," I reflected on the inevitability of change and how it reshapes us. Each of these pieces represents a distinct chapter in my own journey, and as I look back, I realize how much they have shaped me.

Yet, this collection is not just mine. It is ours. It is a reflection of the shared human experience—the universal truths of love, heartbreak, and resilience. You, the reader, may see pieces of your own story within these words. You may have walked paths similar to mine or perhaps, paths that were entirely different but equally poignant. I hope that as you read through these poems, you find solace, understanding, or even the courage to confront your own emotions.

A Note to The Reader

Thank you for walking this journey with me. I cannot express enough how deeply I appreciate your time and attention. These poems are not just my voice; they are an invitation for you to reflect on your own experiences. I hope they have sparked something in you—whether that be joy, sorrow, or a sense of connection. May you continue your own journey with courage, knowing that you are not alone in the ebbs and flows of love and loss.

Recommended Reading

If the themes of love, loss, and self-reflection resonate with you, I recommend reading works by poets and writers such as Rainer Maria Rilke, Pablo Neruda, William Butler Yeats, and Sylvia Plath. Each delves deep into the complexities of the human heart and soul. Additionally, the works of contemporary poets like Lang Leav and Warsan Shire may offer a modern take on similar themes.

About The Author

I am, at heart, someone who has always found solace in words. Writing has been my refuge, my therapy, and my way of understanding the world. I do not claim to have all the answers to the complexities of love and life, but through poetry, I have found a means to navigate their tumultuous terrain. This collection represents my ongoing journey of self-discovery, and I am honoured to share it with you.

Acknowledging The Journey: Final Gratitude

As I bring this collection to a close, I want to express my deepest gratitude to you, the reader. Without you, these words would not have found their place in the world. To those who have supported me, shared their stories, and inspired these poems, I thank you for your presence in my life. Your experiences, your love, and your wisdom have made this journey possible.

To the memory of all those I have loved and lost, this book is for you. To the moments of pain and joy, of silence and noise, thank you for shaping me into the writer I am today.

And lastly, to my own heart—thank you for continuing to feel, to love, and to live through it all.

With love and gratitude,

Charu Gupta (Author)

Akshi Gupta (Co-author)